T0082507

Living Together
—but—
Not Together

Tomiczek

authorHOUSE®

AuthorHouse™
1663 Liberty Drive
Bloomington, IN 47403
www.authorhouse.com
Phone: 1 (800) 839-8640

Published by AuthorHouse 05/05/2017

ISBN: 978-1-5246-9016-8 (sc)
ISBN: 978-1-5246-9015-1 (e)

Library of Congress Control Number: 2017906622

Print information available on the last page.

Contents

Preface

I have always wanted to write a book. This book about my life will hopefully empower and connect with other women and parents who have gone through situations similar to those I've experienced. I can't be the only one. Where do I start?

I was born in Sydney, Nova Scotia, Canada. I moved to Brantford with my parents when I was 3. I grew up there. I had a pretty normal life. My brother and sister are much younger than me. I went away to university and then later moved to Mississauga, a suburb outside of Toronto. I currently live in my hometown with my two children. I am passionate about helping parents who have children with behavioural problems. I am a certified life coach. My website is www.reikiclarisse.wix.com/reiki.

This book is about the struggles and triumphs I have faced and currently face as a mother who has a special needs child. I chose the title *Living Together but Not Together* as a symbolic explanation for what it is like to have a child with special needs. Everyone from the outsides sees the family as living together, but behind closed doors it does not feel like the family is together. No matter how hard I try to connect with my son, there will always be some sort of disconnected, isolating feeling that comes from having a special needs child. This book will explain my life from the beginning of my marriage to the present day.

My Marriage (1999–2005)

I met my husband through a friend when I was in university. We knew each other for about two years before we started dating. We dated for a year and decided that we needed to not be long distance anymore. I was the one who ended up sacrificing. I gave up my job to relocate to his city—a sign of what was to come.

In my new city, I found a job with a non-profit company working with adults with acquired brain injuries. This city was very big compared to what I'd been used to. I was overwhelmed with learning a new job, getting used to a new city, and starting over. I felt that this man did not appreciate the sacrifices that I'd made. Our relationship started becoming strained, and one of my colleagues told me some devastating news about him hitting on her and referring to me as his ex when we were still together. We had a dramatic breakup. I felt used, abused and manipulated.

I was depressed and tried to make the best out of the situation. I wanted to see and enjoy my new city. I tried to embrace being close to Toronto. I went to see *Mamma Mia* with my mom and *The Lion King* with my sister and went to a Leafs' game with my dad and brother on Valentine's Day. I was promoted at work to a team-leader position, which involved writing behaviour programs and managing clients' care. I also became a group leader, which was very fulfilling. I took on a part-time hospital job on a behaviour unit that was toxic but paid well. So I sucked it up.

A year went by, and I reconnected with my ex. He was charming and returned a suitcase I needed for a trip I was taking to the Dominican Republic. He brought me a coffee, and one thing led to another; there we were, dating again. (I like to think I am a strong person, but I have weak moments when I don't make good choices.) I talked myself into believing that this guy came back into my life for a reason—that maybe we'd needed that break to realize what we wanted.

We moved in together, and after a year, we got a condo townhouse. We stayed there for two and a half years. During the time in the condo, we got engaged. Very romantic story. We planned a day trip to New York City, and he proposed on top of the Empire State Building. Sounds great. I told myself, *There is no such thing as the one who blows your mind or sweeps you off your feet.* I made myself believe I was living in a fairy-tale world, hoping to meet my knight in shining armor. I told myself, *I am stupid to let a guy who loves me so much slip away.* I never really felt attracted or drawn to him. He felt safe. I realize now that many guys are charming at first—they like the thrill of the chase—but when it comes to long-term commitment, if they know they have you, their efforts decrease and expectations rise. Many don't even know they are doing this. We women tolerate it because it comes so gradually, almost naturally, that we either learn to accept it or look elsewhere to be and feel appreciated.

Two years later, we got married on the Mayan Riviera. My dad had a ministroke prior to the wedding; in hindsight, that too was a sign. I resigned from my full-time job working with adults with acquired brain injuries and tried doing some private work and work with the autism population. After some time, I realized how challenging autism is and was impressed that the youth I worked with were so intelligent. I accepted a great opportunity to run a day program at a mental health facility. I oversaw the recreation programs run by the volunteers and developed and facilitated psychosocial groups, including anger management, stress management, healthy relationships, conflict resolution, anxiety reduction and sense of self. I really enjoyed the job. It was meaningful work.

My husband and I went for counselling a few times throughout our marriage. It helped for a little while before we fell back into old patterns. We stayed together for convenience, not because we loved each other. I started becoming cold and withdrawn.

My Son in the Beginning (2006–2007)

I became pregnant with my son two years after my wedding. My pregnancy was normal. I didn't like drinking milk from a bag; it tasted like the inside of cow's stomach—which is kind of how my son thinks, and it sounds like something he would say. I also remember feeling very hot, like I was overheating, and symbolic of my son's temper. I was quick to anger and blamed it on hormones. My son's birth was traumatic: 20 hours of back labor and an emergency C-section. He had minor swelling of the brain and was meconium.

When I had my son, I needed to let go of my jobs because I could not do both after my maternity leave. I'd learned so much from my job and was deeply touched by the individuals there. It was hard to leave. As parents, we make so many sacrifices to do what is best for our children. In hindsight, I was meant to stay at the hospital job in West Park. The job gave me the flexibility and freedom to help my child with extra support for his special needs. He was kept in the intensive care unit for three days. It was hard to leave the hospital without him. After two days, he was moved to the children's unit, where I was able to stay with him. I remember arriving at the hospital to find my son was unattended. The nurse watching him had gone on break. I was upset that anyone could have walked off from my son. We were put in a room across from someone in isolation. That person's visitors kept the door open and constantly talked in the doorway. It was not as if the hospital didn't have any empty rooms and that was the only choice. I really wanted to go home.

I had a hard time with nursing because of being separated from my son. I took this hard and experienced terrible postpartum depression with little support. My baby showed intense signs of anger at such a young age. He clenched his fists, and his face turned deep red when he cried. His crying was very loud and alarming. There was no fussing or warning before he went into that intense state at a higher frequency compared to the other babies. Due to his intense behaviour, he was kept in the hospital to rule out medical issues. I asked for his and my hospital records and observed that the notes taken during the delivery stated that I wanted a C-section. This was not true. The heart monitor had made a funny sound, and that is when I was informed that I would be having the procedure.

I felt paranoid. What were they trying to cover up? Where did they go wrong that they needed to lie in the reports? This was the first of many institutions I felt let down by. These people didn't care about my son; they only did the bare minimum.

My son had neonatal follow-up appointments every month to assess his development. Dealing with his day-to-day behaviour and getting him to and from the appointments was emotionally draining and overwhelming. I worried about him misbehaving in public while everyone watched me deal with him and the unwanted attention. Wondering if they would find anything I had to worry about during those appointments created a lot of anxiety. I kept thinking how unfair it was that other mothers could be at home enjoying their babies without having to go to appointments like ours.

Everyone kept thinking I was overreacting. Every time I went to the appointments, I could see that staff were undermining me, thinking I was overexaggerating about his temper. I knew something was different. I told the nurses my concerns regarding his temper, but they never took me seriously. When I explained situations, the staff was very quick to brush it off and downplay it instead of addressing my concerns. I even caught one staff member smirking at another staff member, which was unnecessary in that situation.

At our very last appointment before he aged out of the program, my son was in the nurse's arms while I filled out papers with the doctor. My son started playing with the light switch, turning the lights on and off. I would normally correct that behaviour right away, knowing it would snowball. Something told me to let it play out so they would see what I was telling them. The nurse allowed him to continue with the lights. The doctor asked the nurse to make him stop playing with the switch, and my son lost it. He protested so loudly that people were coming out of their offices to see what was going on. At that point they finally understood what I had been saying. I remember how sad I felt that they had to see my son's outburst to understand what I was dealing with instead of taking my word for it. Very disempowering as a woman, a professional in the behaviour field and, most importantly, as a mother. Not to mention how unfair it was to my son.

They made a referral to another agency and did not tell me. The referral was lost in the shuffle, and we were without support for one and a half years. I got a call from the agency the referral was sent to when my son was three and a half and I was eight months pregnant with my daughter. I was disappointed in the system, which was supposed to be there to help families. The only thing the agency did was give my son a 54-month screening that helped in making his ADHD diagnosis. No guidance or direct support was given. No respite or counselling support was offered, which was what is desperately needed by families who have a special needs child. I thought, *Wow. I'm in the field and I don't know what is happening.* I couldn't imagine how overwhelming it must be for other parents without the knowledge or behaviour experience I had. I didn't even know the right questions to ask. The agency asked questions about my son's findings from the previous program. I did not know at the time I could request their notes, which listed their findings. They did not discuss that with me. Now I know to get copies of notes from agencies involved with his care. I felt like information was hidden from me; many parents don't know it's their right to ask. That was needed when the next agency works with your child.

At School

My son started full-day kindergarten. I was happy to get a break from him and have some alone time with my daughter. With school came a whole new set of issues. I learned how differently he was behaving and the severity of his behaviour in comparison to the other children. I was disappointed with the assessments and lack of support the schools and other agencies provided. My son had undergone a 52-month screening that earmarked him as having ADHD. I was sad when the diagnosis was given to me, which surprised me because I thought I would have been relieved to have answers. The fact was I was scared and not ready for the answer. I was scared that this little person needed so much, and I did not know if I could help him and make the right decisions for him and his future. I didn't know where to start. All I knew was I did not want to screw him up. I put a lot of pressure on myself, to the point I was overwhelmed. I did a lot of personal reflection and growth and realized that my life path, which had previously led me to work in the behavioural field, was to be a better mom for this child who needed me. I had never completely understood why I was in that field, because I really did not want to work with behaviour, but I had needed that experience in order to help my son, this soul who was sent to me.

I gave him my everything. I was constantly correcting or praising him, trying not to enable him. I realized I could not be the mother I thought I wanted to be. He needed structure and constant limit-setting. It made living under the same roof as my son and his father more intense. I did not realize this until I went on a trip to Nova Scotia with my mom and my son to attend a cousin's wedding. It felt like home. I was calm and relaxed for the first time in a long while. I was five months pregnant with my daughter then. I remember thinking life does not need to be as difficult as my life with my husband is. Being in Nova Scotia felt real, peaceful and genuine; I belonged and wanted to stay. When I came back, my husband was all about my son's third birthday party and the house and material things—all superficial stuff. I remember thinking how fake and phony the world I was living in was. I did not want that life. I did not belong there.

When my son started school, I was relieved and could not wait for the break. I always felt guilty that I looked forward to breaks from him, more so than other women from their kids. It made me feel like I was a weak mother. I felt desperate, waiting for the opportunity when I could just sit calmly either by myself or with my daughter.

I experienced all the normal mother's guilt from having a second child. I felt bad that my daughter did not get all my attention as my son had for the first three and a half years of his life. As a feminist at heart, I was sensitive to enforcing that she had the same opportunities as my son. If I felt my son was dominating, monopolizing or manipulating a situation, I was very quick to shut it down. If I saw him exhibiting his father's traits, I was very quick to respond. I was fighting nature without accepting that was how my son was.

In my son's first week in school he was sent to the principal's office for kicking his teacher. When I enquired about the situation (it was not brought to my attention until weeks later) I was given a very vague description of what had happened prior to the situation. The teachers left out how they might have contributed to my son's outburst, and the focus was more on the behaviour than what led to the behaviour. Every person who works in the behaviour field knows there is a reason why behaviours occur; discovering and trying to correct that will eliminate that behaviour. My son was earmarked right away as being a behavioural child. This categorization broke my heart. Like any mother, you want the best for your children. No mother wants to hear her child being talked about and judged unfairly. I never kept any information from the teachers. I was very open about his behaviour. I did not want people taking his behaviour personally. I wanted them to know he could not help it. The school offered to do an informal assessment on him, which determined he had ADHD, which combined hyperactive impulsivity and inattention.

Switching Doctors

At that time, we also switched doctors. Our family doctor was very insulted that I asked for a referral to a pediatrician (this time I gave the name of the one I wanted). I had to switch doctors because this doctor was not helping or taking us seriously. I needed a doctor that would help us move forward and take what I said seriously. I learned from past experiences with this doctor that if I let her choose (as I did when switching over to a gynecologist when I was pregnant with my son) she would give me whoever was available, usually one no one wanted, which was why that doctor was available. Good doctors have waiting lists.

I was angry that she was upset. I thought, *Who is she to be angry? Is she living with the trauma of having a behaviourally challenging child every day?* She downplayed what we went through, not giving us help or answers, and now was offended that I wanted a second opinion. Years later this family doctor discharged my kids and I because we had not had an appointment with her in a year. The office did not contact us to let us know of their new policy, so there we were, in the middle of flu season with no doctor. She did not make enough off us, I guess. In Canada family doctors are paid for visits and intervention.

The pediatrician was progressive and ruled out all other disorders. He made a referral for an autism assessment, which led to my son's diagnosis of being borderline autistic when my son was five. He scored right on the cusp. The developmental pediatric doctor said she could go either way with this. I asked if we could keep the diagnosis and reassess in one to two years and see if he was simply emotionally immature. She agreed. At the second assessment, when my son was seven, she stated she was keeping the diagnosis for him. Once my son had a diagnosis, it was easier to get help and support for him. A team of people supported my son and his teachers. The team consisted of child and youth worker, autism teacher, social worker, special needs coordinator and an occupational therapist as needed. He was put on an individual education program (IEP) in junior kindergarten. An IEP document is developed for each child in public school who needs special education accommodations.

I think the hardest part in all of this was not knowing what I was dealing with. Now I finally had some answers. I still wonder if he had a minor brain injury from brain swelling when he was born, but I chose not to sedate him for an MRI. I just wanted him to have support for dealing with his behaviours, especially at school. I had to play the game by getting him diagnosed—I had to be alert, strategic and agenda focused to get maximal results. It took me years to realize that.

How a Child with Special Needs Affects the Family

My husband has a milder form of ADHD. He believed my son's behaviour was normal because it appeared normal to him. He was in denial and did not support natural remedies I used as a replacement for medication. My husband took medication like it was nothing and did not see why we just didn't take the easy way out and put my son on medication. I wanted to know in good faith that I'd tried and exhausted all other options before turning to medications. That was a last resort for me; if my son were suicidal or school was affected, then I would consider medication. I really struggle with the medication issue because at times I second-guessed whether I was really making the right choices. I hated seeing him suffer and struggle and losing out or missing out on things other children got to experience, like birthday parties. It broke my heart, and I often wondered if I was imposing my own beliefs on him. What was right for him? I wanted to make life easier for him, but the long-term effects and side effects of medication scared me. I prayed to god that I was making the right choice. There were days when I wanted to throw in the towel and put him on medication, but my heart always suggested I should not give up. He needed me to be strong. So I struggled through it with him.

Activities for Special Needs Children

My dear friend suggested that martial arts might help him, so I enrolled my son in kung fu for two and a half years. It was very therapeutic for him. He learned about spacial awareness, body/self-awareness, discipline, respect and focus.

He also received treatment from a reputable Sifu who was also a Chinese doctor. Sifu is the head of the Kung fu school. The treatment consisted of acupuncture and working with qi (energy). It all helped a little to keep him calm.

I was also seeing a naturopath. He recommended a hair test to identify if there were any deficiencies or higher than normal levels of minerals in his body. My son had above-normal levels of aluminum and deficiencies of iron, calcium and magnesium, so I made dietary changes.

We did light therapy with him, which helped significantly and cost a lot of money. The light therapy helped detoxify and break up protein in the lymph nodes. I was worried about the long-term effects of the light therapy. I could not find a lot of information on long-term effects and believed the naturopath was not going to discredit the service; after all, it was their business. My son and I started fading the treatments out (his father felt we were wasting money). I noticed my son relapsed a little.

I started looking at other natural options and tried ayurvedic medicine, which was also recommended by my dear friend. Aruyvedic medicine is the oldest medicine in the world and is made from plants. My son was very resistant towards the Indian head massages given by myself or the ayurvedic doctor. He became very resistant towards taking the herbs as well. My son wanted to try soccer, so we enrolled him in a house league. He picked up the sport very quickly, and it was a perfect fit for him.

One day we got a call from the school that my son was misbehaving and we needed to pick him up. I was angry with my son and the school for not being able to work this out. I was on my way to work, so my husband had to leave work early to get him. The principal stated that if my son was not able to handle full days, we might need to look at him continuing for half days. I told him that was not an option. I would grieve that decision, because my son was not going backwards to make the teachers' and principal's job easier. I also gave feedback to the teacher. I made him aware of his role in my son's escalating behaviour. I was fortunate that this teacher was open enough to receive my feedback, as many teachers were not. This made me realize there was a strong need for behavioural training in schools for the teachers. At that point I almost considered stopping the ayurveda herbs and putting him on medication. He did a quick turnaround when I threatened to pull him out of that school if it happened again. Because his behaviour improved after that point, I did not pursue medication and continued with ayurveda herbs.

An opportunity presented itself for my son to try out for a rep soccer team, and he made it. I was so proud of him. I made a deal with him that if he made the rep team he could take a break from kung fu; he wanted to quit after doing it for two and a half years. I could tell his self-esteem had been boosted. He was beginning to be a normal little boy. At times when playing with other boys at a higher skill level, he was hard on himself. I always tried to remind him to recognize how far he had come and developed. Not many people can say they started a sport at the beginning of the year and ended on a rep league at the end of the year.

After a year and a half of taking the ayurveda herbs, he refused to take them. I had to get tough. I threatened to pull him out of soccer, which I did not want to do because I knew it was therapeutic for him. I was desperate and saw the slow, steady changes in him. I also noticed a relapse in his behaviour after a week of not taking them. The thing with ayurveda medication is that it takes a long time (years) but gets to the root of the problem and to heal the problem. I was able to get him back on the herbs. A month after that, his herbs ran out, and it was hard to get the herbs again. This break made me lose momentum with my son, and he refused to take the herbs again. I couldn't force him to take them. I didn't have control over setbacks like this. I just needed to accept it and make the best of the situation.

Support Services

Behavioural services are agencies that provide staff to come to your home and help parents, caregivers or teachers. They hear about your situation and offer strategies and support. I asked the worker if she could work with my husband and my son's teacher so we could all be on the same page with my son and have some consistency. I was very disappointed by the service. She normalized my husband's responses to my son's behaviours. He manipulated her by saying he didn't have any behaviours with my son because he doesn't put any demands on my son, which he failed to say. He let my son watch TV and play on his Play Station or iPad while he lay on the couch. He let the kids destroy the house, not getting them to pick up after themselves or empty their school bags. So I look like the mean parent when I ask them to do these things. She said there was nothing she could do—another example of an institution only doing the bare minimum.

The reason I was not involved with this agency was because I felt like she was going to tell me what I already knew, like the agency before. That agency had worked mainly with ADHD and had informative workshops, and the worker would come to the house. I realized that because I had not been there, my son had slipped between the cracks.

When I was there, I noticed my ex-husband was not paying attention because there was an underlying expectation I would take care of it. I was stuck between a rock and a hard place, which closely resembled my life with the two of them.

Children Services called on me when my son was in junior kindergarten. He was jumping on the couch. I told him to stop as he was accident prone. Even regular children have been known to break an arm after jumping on the couch. He continued, so I picked him up; his legs dragged off the couch. He said, "Ouch." I saw that he had a scrape under his arm I touched when I picked him up. He said, "You hurt me." The scratch was there prior to me touching him. He thought I hurt him because I touched that sore area. I never thought to address the issue with him as he was always getting scratches. The next day at school the teacher was helping my son put his coat on, and he told the teacher that I'd hurt him. When I went to get my son, he was in the office. The principal told me she could not release him to me and that she had called Children's Aid Society on me. My heart sank, and I was speechless. I felt like my soul had been ripped out from me. How dared they call Children's Aid Society on me? Did they know what I and my son had gone through? Did I look like someone who would hurt my child? Did I fit the profile of parents involved with Children Services? I worked with a vulnerable population and had to report suspected abuse or neglect. It was hard not to take this personally after how hard I had worked with this child. I was the one being abused. I felt that calling Children's Aid Society could have very easily backfired. If that happened now what happened then? My son would have used that to his advantage. For a long time, I was scared to discipline my son, as it might lead to being physical at times. This was not good situation to be in. It was funny how his father could be physical with him and he was scared, but he mocked me. There were times I wished he was not in my life because it was very frustrating and heartbreaking. I felt like the worst mom in the world for feeling this way about my child.

My Spiritual Transformation

Ten days before my son's first birthday, my dad had a massive heart attack and died. He was behind the wheel in his parked van in a parking lot; my mom was in the passenger seat. She was traumatized by the experience and still, to this day, blames herself for not calling the ambulance fast enough. I got the call at work, and that call changed my life forever. I was in shock, mentally paralyzed—I felt like time stood still. I knew I needed to leave and go to Brantford immediately. I drove home, and my ex-husband and I drove to Brantford. I saw my mom and sister out in front of the hospital and ran towards them; we cried and held each other. They brought me inside, where my dad lay peacefully on the bed. I held his left hand—it felt so cold. I couldn't believe he was dead.

I apologized for all my moodiness and bitchiness during the previous year and my attitude towards him. I had been overwhelmed and suffering from postpartum depression. It was not me. I fought hard to get out of it; I was scared it would suck me right back into a downward spiral. But my dad seemed to be watching from above and gave me the strength and calmness to plan, to take charge of his funeral and obituary arrangements and help deal with his estate. To this day, I do not know how I could have done it otherwise. But I kept hearing his voice saying, "It will be okay; just breathe."

A while after I got my mom settled with some support, I decided to start helping myself with my grief. I saw a book called *Talking to Heaven* by James Van Praagh. I felt drawn to it and started reading it. I became interested in mediums and started researching mediumship and how to connect with spirit. I took online classes and was able to do spirit and psychic readings. A dear friend who was deeply into spiritualism told me that my son had 60 percent spirit/psychic awareness and I had 30 percent. This was the journey of my spiritual transformation through becoming more consciously aware. This transformation helped keep me calm and made me feel alive inside. I became very close with this individual. I learned a lot from him. He influenced me and transformed me spiritually. I felt very drawn to him. His voice would vibrate through my soul. It felt like home. I told a coworker I highly respected that I was going to see a medium. She disclosed that she was a medium. She became my mentor, my rock and support. I became very close with her as well. She taught me many things. I aspired to be like her. She was able to give me details about my dad's passing that my mom later confirmed. My dad communicated with her. I desperately wanted to communicate with him. I missed him terribly. A year after his passing I started taking a reiki course. I'd had chronic back pain since my son's delivery. It was excruciatingly painful getting out of bed or bending over to fasten my son's jacket. A few people had suggested I have reiki done. I researched it and decided to do the course so I could do it on me, my son and others every day. Taking that course helped me heal my back pain, put me in a better place mentally and emotionally and gave me my daughter after two years of trying to conceive her. I call her my reiki baby.

My Daughter

After two years of trying to conceive my daughter. I became pregnant with my reiki baby. I had a difficulty pregnancy with her. After an amniocentesis I was bedridden for two weeks. Turned out to be a false reading—another disempowering moment. I remember thinking, *Why are they putting women through this when there are so many high false readings?* There is not enough research to make pregnancy comfortable for women. Trying to swallow huge horse pills they call prenatal vitamins was torturous in itself especially when I was nauseated.

She came three weeks early. I switched hospitals because I wanted to have the same OB doctor and not be rotated. I didn't want another bad experience with my daughter's delivery as I'd had with my son. I had a competent doctor who was on it and took no risks. What should have been a scary experience was a beautiful one. My daughter was extremely tiny at five pounds, and she had the most soulful heart-wrenching cry. I was successful with nursing her. She brought and continues to bring calmness to me. I love her very much, and I am so grateful to have her. She is truly a blessing. A gift from god.

My Son Before the Move

My son would charge at me if I took away his iPad, leaving me with scratches and bruises from blocking his attacks. I worked with another agency as a last-ditch effort. I was really getting tired of trying. The agency worked with autism and behaviour and would come into the home and work with the parent and child on emotional regulation issues. She was my last hope, and I was hoping she could help my son look at situations differently. He was eight and starting to be more self-aware. I was hoping she could reinforce what I had been coaching him about all his life for managing his emotions.

My son had a hard time with connecting with the other boys on the soccer team and struggled with the concept of team and politics within the sport. I felt inadequate at times when coaching him through that as I did not play a competitive sport and was not a boy. His father was not much help in this department either. I started realizing I did not have enough faith and trust in him. I thought he made the team because the coach felt sorry for him because of his diagnosis, but he made the team because they saw something in him. Many of the parents couldn't believe he'd just started soccer a year earlier.

I started recognizing the politics of the game when one of the parent coaches withheld information about a free goalie clinic once a week. I asked her about when it was starting up again; she said it stopped. I said I'd heard it was starting up again, and then she said that she could only choose a few boys. She allowed my son to go. My son really excelled in the goalie position after attending a few clinics. I was kicking myself for not finding out about it earlier, only to find out that it was hidden.

As I wrote this book, I couldn't help thinking how scary and exciting it felt to start a new life with just my kids and me. I hoped I would be happier in my new home but I was also afraid that I would not be able to manage my son by myself or be financially okay. As I decluttered the house and got ready to stage it, it felt very therapeutic. Throwing away memories both good and bad felt like a release; I was moving forward. I threw out five bags of my ex-husband's clothes and felt lighter, like I could breathe again. I experienced mixed emotions and sadness but hoped that it would get better. I felt sad that a chapter of my life had ended but hopeful that the next chapter would be better. It felt good to let go and be sure that I was doing the right thing. I just hoped my kids would be okay. I really dreaded telling them. I couldn't live like that anymore, and my ex-husband did not want to compromise.

My Wishes

I really would have loved to take the kids on a vacation. We went on a family vacation to Nova Scotia when my daughter was 18 months old and my son was 5 years. My ex-husband had never been there before. We drove, which was a lot of work, but I made sure to not take it all on myself. I put ear phones on when it was my turn to drive so my ex-husband would have no choice but to deal with the kids. We fought a lot on the way there, but I stood my ground and he eventually chilled out. I missed my dear friend. I texted him any chance I could to give him updates about our trip. I sent him pictures.

When my son was in grade three, he had an awesome teacher and enjoyed soccer. We continued to have good days and bad days, but my son was steadily getting better. His teachers from kindergarten and grade one and other people who knew him in his earlier years were amazed at the difference in his demeanor, which was good and uplifting— what I needed to hear.

The Separation

At the time my husband and I were separating, my son's behaviours were getting worst. He was more confrontational, more defiant and becoming more difficult to manage. My husband didn't want to stay together because of the kids. I wanted to stay because of the kids. I worked so hard to get my son better that I couldn't bear seeing him regress. We had made so many behavioural gains with him that it broke my heart to see him regress to where he had been years before. So that was it; 18 years together was gone. I no longer loved this man the way he wanted and needed me to. I had nothing left to give. All I had went to my children. I wanted to be left alone, and I felt unlovable. I felt like the world was against me. No one understood what is was like to be in my situation. I felt like I gave and sacrificed but did not get back nearly what I put in. Story of my life.

The people who were close to me let me down so many times that I started withdrawing from them. I realized it was just me and my kids. I had no one else. I was told by a mutual male friend that guys need to hit rock bottom to realize what they have. Hearing that made me feel like I did not want to be with a man if they were all like that. Right before listing our house, my husband asked if I was sure about separating. I couldn't believe he decided to tell me he was not sure and that he still loved me. I told him I needed this from him five years earlier. I couldn't make myself fall in love with him after all he put me through. It also made me mad that it had to come to that before he appreciated me. He wouldn't change, he couldn't. That was who he was. I know I hurt him. He started crying, and then I started crying. I felt horrible; I didn't want to hurt anyone. I just couldn't lie to him. The thought of living with him made me feel sick. I asked if he could live in the basement for time being as a compromise. He said no; he wanted to work on us. I felt like there was no compromising except for me, who was expected to compromise again.

That was not the life I wanted anymore. I don't want a one-sided relationship anymore. I would compromise for my kids. I felt bad for hurting him, but I realized he did not feel bad for hurting me all these years. I do not think he really wanted to make it work or that he truly loved me; he just was complacent and comfortable. I made his life convenient. He was scared about living on his own, away from his family. He had never done that before. He'd lived at home until he lived with me. I just wanted to get away from it all. Maybe I would have the strength to better deal with my son. I had been told to stay with my husband until the kids were older; I would not be able to handle my son on my own. He would not turn out well if I didn't sacrifice. That advice scared me and kept me in a place of despair for two and a half years. One friend shook her head and told me that I would be healthier living apart from my ex-husband. In my heart, I knew I needed to go. The situation was cancerous, and my health was declining. I felt dead inside. I'd sacrificed enough.

When we told the kids about separating, my 5-year-old daughter was confused, and my 9-year-old son starting crying. It was heartbreaking. The child had been through enough. We sold the house, which was on the market for five days. It was not as stressful as I thought it was going to be. Our realtor had a cleaner and stager come in to get our house ready to list. All I had to do was declutter, and my ex-husband did some touch-ups. The most stressful part was that my ex-husband constantly watched what I was doing when he needed to be concerned with what he needed to be doing. He was constantly comparing and rebelling about who was doing more work. That validated why I did not want to be with him.

I rented a garbage bin, and we filled it with in three days. I could not believe the crap we'd collected in 12 years. Mostly it was his stuff. A purger living with three hoarders, I'd obviously lost the war. We worked hard and received ten thousand dollars over the asking price. I bought a beautiful house in Brantford I had to fight for. I felt like I was being screwed over by my realtor there, but once I voiced my concern he changed his game plan. This was my life now as a single mother. I need to set limits and boundaries and call people out on being unfair. No one else is going to fight for me and my kids. It was time to be strong.

Meeting with the lawyer to review the separation agreement, I became very emotional. I had not expected the lawyer to tell me how much I was being screwed over with child support payments. I explained that was the condition my ex-husband set to allow us to move to Brantford. I could not afford a nice place for the kids in Mississauga. I would have been stuck in a crappy townhouse in a crappy neighbourhood. I could at least give them a good home in a good neighbourhood in Brantford and get little support from my mom. That arrangement worked. I could be home with my kids during the week, and he could take the kids on the weekends, which would allow me to commute to work. The lawyer almost refused to sign the agreement, insisting I was entitled to more than two hundred a month for both children. He told me I could easily get a thousand dollars a month. He stated that my ex-husband's lawyer must wonder how he'd got me to agree to this. The lawyer made me feel like a fool and got me riled up. He went on to say I should have received more of his pension plan. I understood his agenda; he wanted me to fight so he received more money. I didn't want to fight. I told him I was not in a financial position to fight the agreement. I understood that I was at a disadvantage in the agreement, but I wanted to cut my losses and move forward. It was not worth the fight.

I didn't want things to get nasty, which might easily have happened. I know my ex-husband's family was advising him to protect himself (both of his brothers were separated), but it meant screwing me over in the end. I had to suck that up and learn from it. I was trying really hard not to let the experience ruin me. I was mad at myself for being so naive and trusting and getting screwed over in the end. The experience toughened me up. I tried to have faith that not all men and their families thought like that. It seemed very disrespectful to be screwed over by people who once called me family, very fake and hypocritical. I had the chance to screw him over, but I never did that. I didn't want that in

31

my karma. As angry and hurt as I was, I was not vicious or manipulative enough to imagine a strategy for screwing someone else over. I was not built like that, and I was happy that I was not. I hoped I could learn to trust the right people in the future. I tried to keep my eye on the end goal: being free of that man and his family.

I had my life coaching certificate, and I was a reiki master, allowing the opportunity to work with clients during the weekdays when the kids were in school to make extra money. Working with other parents who had experienced being a parent for a child with special needs was my life's passion. I had a dream of running a support group for parents and their ADHD children. When no one wants their children to play with your children or to babysit your child, it is very isolating.

Days after our house was sold, my neighbour disclosed to me that her 34-year-old son had ADHD. The stories she told me were mirror images of what I went through with my son. It was therapeutic to talk with someone who understood what it was like. I hoped to have her as a guest speaker at the support group. I imagined other guest speakers I would invite for educational purposes. I pictured hosting a group of both parents and kids once a month, depending on demand. I visualized an educational first hour and support during the second hour. I knew that journey would be healing for me and my kids too.

The Move

The stress from my job was becoming unbearable. Everyone was fighting. New management was listening to the wrong people and making stupid decisions. I hoped to not need that job. I was hoping to get my mortgage paid off or down so I would not feel trapped there, as it paid well. I didn't belong anymore in Mississauga, West Park. I needed to learn to be alone. Sometimes I felt unlovable and that maybe I was not meant to be with anyone. I hoped I would make some new friends and reconnect with old friends. It was hard to maintain the friends I had, a common experience for parents with behavioural kids, isolated from parents who did not want their kids around your kids. I often felt drained after being with my son, with no energy left to put towards maintaining a friendship. It was sad and unhealthy. I hoped that would change when we moved. Smaller towns have a better sense of community, and I was hoping they would accept me and my kids. My ex-husband was not a social being, which made it difficult to reconnect with friends. It honestly was not worth the fight. So I stayed home to keep the peace. It's funny; my dear friend would say how spoiled I was, that I could do all the things I wanted, but in fact I had to fight for those things. I made many sacrifices, putting others before me. I was trying not to do that anymore. My kids were the only people coming before me now.

I felt like no one was looking out for me, so I needed to be careful. I felt I had no one; it was just me and my kids. I hoped this move will also help me reconnect with my mom again. Our relationship had become a little strained after I had my son. I felt like I'd become an edgier, no-nonsense person. Reiki helped soften me. How had my life become such a mess, like it was falling apart at the seams? I prayed every day to have the strength to get through it. I hoped to be a strong, positive influence on my children. I didn't want to let them down.

Before the Move

Forty-five days before moving day, the stress was building. My son's behaviours were becoming more frequent and more intense. He was starting to act out. My ex-husband played games, changing his mind and screwing me over in the process. My daughter became more withdrawn. I hoped I had not failed my kids. I couldn't stay stuck in this toxic relationship with my ex-husband.

Once I had to pull over to the side of the road to restrain my son and received multiple big bruises. It was the worst I had ever experienced with him. My hair was falling out. I was making a mess of my relationship with my dear friend. It felt like everything was falling apart, no matter how much I tried to fix, make better or avoid fights. They were coming at me from all angles, draining me. I struggled to keep my head above water. What had I done to deserves this? I felt very unlovable and withdrew from the world. I was scared of being alone, but who was going to want me, with a child with special needs? I worried that if I met someone he would not share the patience and love I have for my son. I worried about pedophiles who watched for single mothers. I needed to be very cautious. I knew I needed to take some time to heal and be there for my kids over the next year. I had been too trusting; now I was very cautious and not trusting, as I had been screwed over one too many times.

Leading up to the move, the tension in the house increased. I felt like my ex-husband was constantly trying to screw me over. First he said he would let me take everything. Then he changed his mind; he wanted the TV and the dining room table, even though his place was fully furnished. He was malicious and spiteful, which confirmed why I did not want to be with him. I tried to work a lot before the move to avoid being around him. He had a way of really dragging me into a dark place. I just tried to focus on my new life in Brantford, the light at the end of the tunnel. He took the laptop without asking me, which was fine because I had already purchased one to start writing this book. Without him knowing, I kept it in my trunk. Pretty sad to be a grown woman and need to hide things.

The standard practice when purchasing a home in Ontario, Canada, is that the buyer is allowed to have two visits prior to the move-in date. My mom came with me on our first visit, when I brought the kids to see the new house. She started asking personal questions of the realtor, who was a family friend. The sellers wore curious looks on their faces. I spoke to my mom about not mentioning that we knew the realtor. She said, "I am not going to live my life worrying about how people take what I say. My intentions are pure. Not my problem how people take what I say. I would rather be dumb and happy than smart and fearful." That summed up the familiarity of a small-town attitude: honest and pure, not strategic or focused on a competitive agenda. I had missed that simplicity in my life and couldn't wait to have it back. What I'd had with my ex-husband had ruined me, but living in a big city made me stronger. I knew the life I wanted to lead. I didn't want fast-paced or cutthroat thoughts; I wanted peace and healing.

The day of the move was stressful. I had to work and could not drop my shift. My ex-husband had the day off, but he was useless. He had moved out a week before and left everything to me to do, which was always the way. He was more a hindrance than a help, which should not have surprised me. He stayed for a few hours afterwards, picking non-stop fights. I left because I needed to board the dog and bring the cat to my mom's. I really needed to be away from him. The movers screwed me over every way possible. They took an extra hour to load things on the truck, which consisted of 12 items that were disassembled and wrapped. When asked why it was taking them so long, they replied, "We don't want to damage anything." But they'd scratched that paint on the wall beside the stairs leading to the basement. They also scratched the paint from the front door and left a brand-new chair, now severely torn, in the garage. They took the long route from Mississauga to Brantford; what should have taken an hour took two hours. At my storage unit, they said they needed to reassemble everything I had in there to make everything fit. There was no reason why they could not stack. I had made sure I'd left enough room for them. They still could not fit everything in. I called their supervisor, but he never returned my calls or answered when I called. It was hard to swallow, but this was going to be my life as a single mother. I needed to be tougher and less trusting.

There was a 12-day delay from when I closed on the old house to when I moved into the new house. I took the kids on a minivacation. There was a lot of fighting and attention-seeking from my son. It was clear he was having a very difficult time coping with this. What I thought would have been a fun trip was too much for my son. It was an eye-opening experience. It was very stressful driving with the two of them fighting. There were a few times he charged at me and I contemplated about putting him on medication. A few people mentioned cannabis oil to me for my son. I researched it but had mixed feelings about being a mother putting my 9-year-old child on cannabis. I read the miraculous reviews from mothers who had put their children with ADHD and autism on it. I held off, waiting to see whether my son was going through a rough patch. If he got better, I would hold off.

I also thought I could continue to put my son into camp for four weeks of the summer. I usually booked two weeks in July and two in August, but the two weeks in August we were in Brantford, and it was too much for him. He wanted to do half days. I was starting to learn to go with his momentum, not what I thought would distract him. I have learned and I am still learning when to push and when to pull back with him. My personality has always been to push and motivate, but I was learning that it was better to sometimes pull back and let things happen naturally at its own pace.

Our New Life

I was starting to feel like I could breathe again. I had my own home, I could parent how I wanted to parent and I had freedom. It was a nice place to be. I was grateful for having my life back. I worked Friday through Sunday at work, which helped me avoid all the silly politics and bureaucracy that went during the week. I could just go in and work with my clients without the stress of people trying to start problems. My life was starting to come together, and I could deal with the stresses of work better. I felt myself healing. I had waited so long to feel stronger and to care for my children. I actually enjoyed my time with them more, and I was more patient. I did not fully realize how much my marriage was taking from me until I was out of that situation.

I had saved some money in case I needed it, so I was very happy that everything had turned out fine. Financially, I just needed to be conscious of my spending. I had always spent money to cope with the pain, but now all I wanted to do was stay home and enjoy my new house. It was beautiful and mine. It was totally to my taste; the other house was more my ex-husband, but this house was more me. I saw signs all around that I'd made the right choice. The tension was gone from the house, and everyone started to settle in. It was a new area with new families and a lot of building going on, which would increase the value of the house. I even knew my neighbours; I used to work with the wife when I first moved to Mississauga. What were the odds? I thought I would miss Mississauga, but I'd never felt like I belonged there. People were not as genuine as they were here. My relationships there did not feel real.

My son had not made any friends yet, and his behaviours increased. The half-day camp was okay, but I really needed full day off. It seemed like he was having more bad days, almost every other day. He kept destroying things around the house, leaving messes everywhere and refusing to clean up after himself. When he started targeting my daughter, that's when I stepped in. He charged at me and tore my favourite shirt. He threw a patio chair, not a great scene for anyone watching. Two days later my new dress was ripped while restraining him, all because he went back on his word about sharing his iPad charger with his sister. I was going to buy her a new one, but he said he would share. When it came time to share he refused, even after I asked nicely. So I held him accountable and I took it. I told my daughter to go charge it downstairs. I held him back when he tried to charge at her a few times. I felt my daughter was not safe so I told her to stay close to me afterwards when he was in his room calming down. It was the longest and worst restraint. He called me a fucking bitch, spit in my face, pulled my hair, scratched and pinched me, kicked and punched me, told me he was going to get a knife and stab me and his sister. I felt ill and knew at that moment I could not control him anymore. I needed help. I was desperate.

So when he was settling down in his room and my daughter was beside me in my room, I called his dad. I told him what the last few days had been like and asked him what his thoughts were on cannabis oil. I sent him a few articles and he agreed. The next morning, I called the doctor to make an appointment.

I was asked to interview for a position in a day program in Brantford. I had completed a co-op placement there as a student 20 years before and remembered how pleasant the atmosphere was. When I picked up my son, I learned my boss's daughter was one of the head counsellors there. That was a sign that I should go check out the interview.

The interview went awesome. I could not have asked for a better interview. The director of care interviewed me, along with her right-wing woman, who I also knew from when I'd volunteered during high school at a nursing home. She had been on staff there. She remembered me right away and gave me a hug. I was immediately given a tour. Lori, the director, told me that she was pretty impressed with my credentials and said I had everything they needed. It was a perfect fit. She wanted me in for training first week of September, which was perfect for me. I'd needed some good news after all that I had been through and was going through with my son, and the experience was very welcoming. I hated to feel trapped. When I was living with my ex-husband, I was trapped in my room when he came home because I could not bear to be in the same room with him. I was trapped at my job, though less so because I worked on the weekends.

I took my son to the doctor the following morning to see what my options were for trying cannabis oil with my son. The doctor said she disagreed with my decision in front of my son. I told her that she was not living with the abuse and torture I had been the last nine years. I read that doctors will not support cannabis oil because it is outside of their pharmaceutical training. She forwarded me on to a marijuana clinic. The doctor who ran the clinic was only in once a week. I thought to myself, *What kind of support is this?* The assistant answered emails and messages once a week and said she was not sure about the laws for cannabis oil with children. I replied I was not aware of restrictions; I had read many miracle stories about children being on it. I told her the other alternative was medication, but I wanted cannabis oil because it has fewer side effects or long-term effects and was natural. The body knew what to do with it. She did not reply. I hoped I could speak with the doctor.

I planned to set up some family counselling. I was hoping that if my son talked to someone objective, it might help him understand how his thoughts affected him. I wanted him to heal and to have a release or outlet. I tried to put him in a physical activity, hoping it would be therapeutic for him. He refused to play soccer or any other sport. He asked to go swimming, so I signed him up for back-to-back lessons through all the levels. I hoped swimming will help settle him.

I knew he was nervous about starting a new school the following week. I hoped and prayed he would make friends and feel supported by his teacher. We arranged to meet the principal the Friday morning before school began. She gave us a tour, and the kids saw their classrooms. I got all their supplies ready and packed. The more I prepare my son, the less anxiety he experiences. I knew the last week before school was going to be difficult for him. He was okay Monday. I took the kids to a huge pool I used to go to as a child, and they loved it. I also took them canoeing and out for lunch. My son had one episode before bed because his iPad would not charge and he was mad that his sister would not give him hers. He kicked her, and her fingers were caught in the crossfire. I spanked him and called him a coward; I told him to pick on someone his own size. I told him if he touched her again he was out of this house.

I knew I'd taken it a little too far. I'd been tired, without energy at the end of the day and looking forward to go to bed. That episode was not what I wanted to hear before going to sleep. I was also upset that after all I did for them that day, that was how he'd acted. It also is not good about his iPad failing, because that was what I used for leverage, taking it away when misbehaved. I felt like I needed to be more creative in my approach to discipline. Unfortunately, that day was not the only day we had trouble. The day before had not been a good day. I took the kids to a mini–water park that they'd loved before. It cost a lot of money, and we had lunch there. My son started acting up after two hours, so we left. I had to stop the car on the side of the road a few times to threaten to throw him out of my car. It worked for 10 minutes. The third time I actually did leave him, which shocked him and me. I was starting to lose it. That was not the kind of mom I want to be. Who had I become? I hated that person I had become. I thought maybe I should go on cannabis oil to help me cope better with him. I was too stressed to handle him anymore. I felt like a failure, like I had let him down. Thank god my mom stepped in and helped me. I dropped my son off on Monday for a few hours, and Tuesday evening she kept him overnight. We needed the break from each other. I think she saw how serious it was when I told her I was ready to give him up to foster care. That was a very low point for me.

The second piece of information I received from the cannabis clinic my son was referred to informed me that Canadian law stated I could not put a child on cannabis oil as a first-line treatment. I needed to put him on medication for a year first. How ridiculous. I needed to make things worse for him before I could make it better because doctors only understand pharmaceutical training. It was a huge letdown. I chose to try cannabis oil after reading miracle stories parents posted regarding their children who used cannabis oil. Many documentaries support the use of cannabis oil for medicinal purposes. I believe parents, who live day to day with the struggles of having a special needs child, over doctors who are paid every time they prescribe a pharmaceutical medication. I was disappointed that doctors did not having enough confidence to try something natural. Especially when I looked at the harsh side effects and long-term effects such medications have. It was heartbreaking.

My other option was to go on the black market for it. I didn't want to put myself or my son in that situation. I was all my kids had and couldn't be doing illegal activities, as desperate as I was. I wanted to blast the doctor and say, "That is why parents turn to the black market—because of the medical system letting them down." I know it was not his fault. He was being paid and trained by pharmaceutical companies and couldn't act against legislation. It was frustrating as a parent to need to resort to making my son worse before I could make him better. It was not fair to him or those of us who must deal with the crap that comes with trying different medications. I wished desperately there was another way.

The Adjustments, September 2016

The kids' first day of school was a success. My son made two new friends. My daughter did too. They seemed happy. I hoped I could get him to go to the emotional regulation group. I hoped he really benefited from it. I had heard great things about it. An emotional regulation group helps children and parents understand the children's strong emotions and how to manage them more effectively. There was a huge awareness and education component to these psychosocial groups.

He had a pediatrician appointment at the end on the month. I hoped he could help. It didn't look too good.

I went to drop off my police background check at the day program job opportunity agency, and they met me right away with Chris (the second in charge), who scheduled me for training shifts. Lori wanted me to facilitate a new acquired brain injury group next month to help them format and plan how they wanted to run this group and what they were hoping they would get out of it. I was really excited to be a part of it. She also wanted me to educate her staff on working with individuals with acquired brain injuries at a staff meeting or at a lunch and learn. It was nice to feel needed and appreciated. She seemed really flexible, which was what I needed. I wanted to not do shift work anymore, which was very inconsistent for both my children.

This career change could help my children settle in more and allow me to work when they were in school. I didn't want to work evenings, because I only had Monday to Thursday evenings with them according to the custody agreement. When I told her what I currently made at the hospital, it was clear that she could not pay me that much, which was fine as long as I earned the same or more by working more hours while the kids were in school. The hours were very compatible with the kids' school schedule. Plus, it involved doing what I like and a better work environment; I would also be closer to my kids. I asked her if we could go slowly, as it would be more natural and better for all involved, and she agreed. I was glad that she and I were on the same page. I discovered after reading their newsletter that the president of the board of directors was my daughters kindergarten teacher. What were the odds? Another sign.

While the kids were in school, I had some much-needed down time. I went for my first orientation training at the day program in the second week of school. It was great, very busy. I got to sit in on groups and watch rehabilitation exercises. I was trained on the paperwork. I was able to meet with the speech and language therapist and the social worker. I provided bank information to be set up on the payroll. I even had the opportunity to do reiki on a caregiver who was in pain.

I was desperately trying to get my son into soccer again. It broke my heart every time I dropped him off and saw him sitting by himself in the schoolyard. I discussed with him later that evening the need to get involved and make friends and said he was spending too much time alone in his room and relying on his sister for friendship. That had been evident when we rode our bikes home from school the day before and went to a park. My daughter had friends, and my son was being rude to her friends. When I called my son out on it, he got mad, and we ended up leaving. He later disclosed that his sister didn't want to play with him; she wanted to play with her friends at school. I supported it and said he needed to start making his own friends. I was proud of my daughter for standing up for herself and expressing what she wanted. I sometimes worried that she was so laid back that my son's strong personality would overpower her.

I told him I wanted to put him into programs so he would meet people. He was upset. He said, "I am suffering enough." I was shocked by his comment because he held so much inside. I didn't want to see him suffer anymore, and I seriously considered trying medications. I planned to bring it up at the pediatric appointment at the end of the month. I also wanted to talk to the teacher and get his input about if my son started tried to connect with others.

I put my daughter in a PA day child-minding service at the school; there was no school on PA days. I wanted her to meet other kids. I also felt that leaving my son and daughter all day with my mom was a little much. My son was much more calm separate from his sister. It also gave me a chance to reconnect with him and have some alone time with him.

Fridays were emotionally hard days for me because I knew I was not going to see my kids until Monday morning. I missed them terribly over the weekends. Even though I need a break from my son, I found myself looking at their pictures, crying and apologizing for putting them through this. I just couldn't stay in a loveless marriage. I felt like I was dying inside.

October 2016

I met with the pediatrician. He seemed very invested and competent in his work. His personality and humour won my son over. He was not a pill pusher, which I appreciated. He himself has a ADHD son, so he understood us. When he asked my son about his parents separating, my son said it was not bad because we didn't fight anymore. I really needed to hear that reassurance, that he saw why this needed to happen. I thought the doctor would be a great support for us; I felt optimistic about us. He was very quick to respond negatively to cannabis oil, so I'm not sure how I felt about that. I also booked an appointment with a naturopath here in Brantford. I wondered if he could write a note to advocate for my son with cannabis oil or give him something natural to help him.

Sometimes I felt like I was fighting the world. I was so frustrated with the lack of support. My case worker for special services at home was changed to a very firm, strict and less helpful worker. These workers were in charge of funding decisions regarding children's needs. When I filled out the extensive paperwork—15 pages to apply for this funding—I did not know specifically what her role included. The worker I had before this worker was very helpful in explaining policies to me. But trying to get information from this worker was like pulling teeth. I applied for children with severe disabilities funding, which I'd received in the past when my ex-husband was laid off; it was based mainly on income. She told me I made too much, so I told her (three separate times over the course of four months) that my income did change. I was a single mother, forced to work fewer shifts due to child care and custody. I had to move to Brantford to afford housing. I was actually making less than when I'd received funding last time, and I'd had no problem getting it last time. This worker made me go back and forth and give her extra documents at least three times. She dragged her heels and delayed responding. After six months, I lost it and contacted her supervisor. I was desperate and frustrated that this government agency was supposed to help people and instead I was being given more stress and grief for trying to get help. I cried and told her I did not ask to have a child with disabilities who I needed to restrain, receiving bruises all over. I was not asking for more than what I needed, and I was being made to feel like I was stealing. It was a pride-breaking moment. The manager finally worked with this worker, and my file was made a priority. It was sad that I needed to break down in order to get the help we need before I was taken seriously. This reminded me of when my son had his meltdown on our last neonatal appointment. The doctor and nurse took us seriously when they saw his behaviour for themselves. My application was granted, with three months' back pay and a little bit a month, which helped significantly.

My son disclosed to me that he was being bullied at school. I left a message in his agenda for the teacher to call me. He was away, so I went straight to the principal. I told her that kids were calling him a princess, and other things, saying he had a vagina. I told her that my son rarely disclosed information, and for him to come to me proved how bad it was. I expressed my concern about his already-low self-esteem and said he had been through a lot. I informed her that if pushed, my son would take the bait, which could very easily escalate to physical violence. I communicated with her that my son might have played a role by calling names back to defend himself. She was on it, and I was impressed.

She went to the class and had a firm talk with the students about name-calling and bullying. She told them that if students came to her she would be more lenient than if she found out. I liked that she made them come to her with names. She sat in on lunch break and observed recesses. She made her presence known and was very in tune with the kids. She discreetly tried to get my son to talk with her, but he wouldn't. When I checked back in with her at the end of the day, she was able to give me names. One child blamed my son for name-calling and told her that a girl was telling everyone my son liked her. The principal knew right away which girl liked that kind of drama. The principal met the girl in the hallway when she was coming back from the washroom and asked her why she was telling everyone that my son liked her. She told the principal that another guy told her that my son told him that. I thanked her for the information. When I picked up my son I praised him for coming to me. I mentioned the names I was told, and he looked surprised that I'd found out. I also warned him to be more careful about who he told personal stuff to. He didn't need to tell people who he liked. I hoped he learned from the experience. He reported no one had targeted him that day, probably because of the principal's presence.

I think my son was trying to connect with boys at school. He brought Lego Ninjovo and Pokémon to trade with. He still refused to play soccer. Both children were swimming, and my daughter did gymnastics. I tried not to push him too hard and gave him space and time to adjust. After a few really rough patches, he seemed to be getting a little better.

November 2016

I tried giving him hemp seed oil in the morning on his pancakes and lavender at night, and I noticed a little change in his behaviour. He seemed more calm and cool, even with all the bullying. Every little bit helped. Hemp seed oil was an alternative to cannabis oil and easier to get. No prescription was needed, and hemp oil was available in many health food stores. I learned about this from a coworker who is a nurse and has a child with autism.

My son's teacher said he was doing well in class and stayed to himself at recess and lunch. When asked why he was not playing with the kids, my son answered that he didn't want to. Seeing him alone broke my heart. I really hoped he'd make a friend.

I signed my son up for an emotional regulation class that met for one and a half hours once a week for eight weeks. I hoped he would benefit. He did a little; it was a stepping stone. We attended our first emotional regulation group. My son refused to go, but I held firm on this decision. He needed to learn how to work with his strong emotions. He refused to participate. Everyone was friendly, and my son started warming up towards the end. He later told me he wanted to participate but didn't want to feel like a dork.

I told him all the other kids were participating. He never responded, but he did participate the following week.

He got a taste of what it was like to attend an educational and insightful self-help group. I attended with him, as required. I wished the organization facilitating the group would fade out the parents in the last half of the eight-week program. I was given numbers to call when I was in a crisis, which I hoped I wouldn't need to use.

My mom reported that she had some difficulties with him after he arrived from his dad's after the weekend. I called the crisis line to see what support we could get for my mom and my son while I was at work. The person I spoke to on the crisis line was useless and not any help.

Two Weeks Later

He participated fully in the course. He seemed to enjoy it and took in what was being taught. They were discussing how to recognize changes in the body to anticipate when their emotions would start becoming strong. Last week they made a relaxation kit and did activities to make them more mindful and get them out of the fight-or-flight state that I thought was brilliant. I liked how they talked about and taught the material in a way kids with ADHD would recognize. They did some mindful activities. I made note of the material so my son could Google it on his iPad. The coping techniques were great. I hoped they would go a little deeper with the material and not just stay on the surface.

Bullying at School

I taught my son how to stand up for himself and set limits with the other kids, and it seemed to be working. I stressed the importance of talking with his teacher on a weekly basis, as I was only getting one side (my son's side) of what was going on, and my son made it seem worse than it was.

I touched base weekly with the teacher for an ongoing dialog to see how my son was doing. The teacher delayed and resisted the touching-base thing, but I persisted, and he finally agreed. I told the teacher that my son felt like he did not care. I think this statement struck a chord in the teacher, triggering his awareness of how he was coming off towards my son and myself. I explained that my son had met with a homeopathic progressive medicine doctor and had prescribed two medicines. I needed to know if the teacher observed any changes in my son's behaviour and focus. I needed that information to know whether he needed something stronger. Homeopathic medicine takes longer to yield results. The general rule was that however long you have had your issue, it takes that many months before you start seeing the medicine's full effects.

Homeopathic Doctor

The doctor was very in tune with my son and me. He was going to check with his college about writing a letter recommending my son could benefit from being on the cannabis oil. I asked whether the medication he was taking was considered a first line of defense, and he said yes. Our game plan was for my son to take the homeopathic medicine for a year. One medication was for calmness, the other for focusing. I asked the doctor if he could prescribe a liquid or chewable form with a pleasant taste, or else my son would not take it. He was able to accommodate that request. If he needed something stronger in the future, this doctor might be able to recommend getting him on cannabis oil if needed. I spoke to his Ayurveda doctor to see whether she would be willing to write a letter as well, stating that my son had been taking her medicine for year and half and would benefit from cannabis oil. She refused.

I talked with my son about the importance of telling me how he felt and whether he noticed that he woke feeling more clear and calm. When I Googled the medication, it explained that the liquid form automatically passed into the bloodstream; I might start seeing subtle changes, but it might take a few weeks for full effects to show. The next morning my son woke up and required no prompting to get dressed and eat his breakfast. I praised him and said that was how it should be in the mornings. Not arguing was a much better way to start off the day. He agreed and told me he thought the medication was working. I let out a sigh of relief. I really hoped he was right.

I communicated with his father about the medication so he would consistently give it to him over the weekend. I touched base with him Sunday evening to see how my son's weekend went. I also told my mom about it, as she needed to give him his after-school dose on Fridays and the bedtime dose Sunday evenings.

The teacher informed me that my son had a very difficult time with the last hour of school. I suggested that he receive some one-on-one support or small group activities to bring his focus back. I also said I would talk with his doctor about moving the after-school focus medication to lunchtime and adding another dose of the calming medication at that time too. He needed stronger calming medication, as he still was not settling at night.

Work and Survival

I could work a minimum of three shifts per week, and they tried to take away a shift because clients were down. That happened because someone was not doing his or her job and making sure we had clients on the wait-list. I fought to keep the shift. I told the staff at the staffing office that it was not fair that I had only five when other part-timers had seven or 10 shifts. She said their shifts were not affected by the decrease in clients. So I was being punished once again for being stuck in a situation that I couldn't control. I told her another staff with less seniority than me should not have had their bare minimum if I didn't and they had shifts I could work. She lied at first and said everyone had shifts taken away. So I investigated and found out she'd lied, and I called her out on it. She finally gave me my shift back. I told her that less than three shifts meant my kids and I wouldn't eat. She didn't care; she just wanted to get the job done as easily as she could. Being a single mom does make you an easy target. No one cares about the stress and struggles you face on a daily basis. Added stresses become a bit much to take.

I talked with the supervisor, letting her know the impact of my shifts being cut meant that my kids and I wouldn't eat and I could lose my house. She was not concerned. I felt so low, disappointed. The woman was a mother, and there was no empathy or concern at all. I even offered to help out with marketing and assessing new clients to help fill our beds faster, and she didn't respond to my e-mail. I knew then I desperately needed to find a new job. I had been there 16 years. I knew I should not have had to fight to keep the bare minimum of shifts there. They did not care about me and my kids.

Towards the middle of November, after applying to numerous jobs, I was finally offered a part-time supervisor position at a residential facility working with special needs adults. The drive to the hospital job was a little taxing, but I felt a huge sense of relief that I would not need to rely on the hospital job anymore. The atmosphere was getting worse, and I knew I needed to start making my way out of there. It was just a matter of time before they closed the unit. I just wanted to still keep my foot in the door for my severance package. They brought in a severely aggressive client we couldn't properly support; people would get hurt. I could not afford to get hurt; I needed to be strong to work my other jobs. I would not get paid if I was hurt. It felt like a setup. I tried to do the bare minimum there and focus on getting reiki clients at the new job and the day program. I hoped to eventually give up the hospital job. I didn't belong there anymore.

Conclusion

My son was receiving respite support twice a week for when my mom watched the children, as my son could be very hard to handle. I needed that so I could feel comfortable at work, knowing my mom had support. The autism agency providing the respite workers also helped me with funding. My son was also on the wait-list for an anxiety reduction class that he is would attend by himself. I felt that was better for him; I was a distraction to him in the emotional regulation workshop. My son would soon start cognitive behavioural therapy sessions with his homeopathic doctor. I heard many good things about this type of one-on-one counselling.

I was offered more guaranteed hours as a supervisor in a group home close to where we lived, which allowed me to let go of the toxic hospital job, reducing my anxieties and making things easier for us. It finally felt like things were starting to come together, the calm after the storm.

Once you have a diagnosis for your child and apply for the funding that child is entitled to, parents can look beyond the free services that usually have long wait-lists.

The more support you can accumulate for you and your child, the more you can focus on the next step for where you want to go.

It does get easier once the supports are in place.

Printed in the United States
By Bookmasters